BOA
EDITIONS LTD

RAIL

RAIL

POEMS BY

Kai Carlson-Wee

❖ ❖ ❖

A. POULIN, JR. NEW POETS OF AMERICA SERIES, NO. 41

BOA EDITIONS, LTD. ❖ ROCHESTER, NY ❖ 2018

First Edition
18 19 20 21 7 6 5 4 3 2 1

For information about permission to reuse any material from this book, please contact The
Permissions Company at www.permissionscompany.com or e-mail permdude@gmail.com.

Publications by BOA Editions, Ltd.—a not-for-profit corporation under
section 501 (c) (3) of the United States Internal Revenue Code—are made
possible with funds from a variety of sources, including public funds from
the Literature Program of the National Endowment for the Arts; the
New York State Council on the Arts, a state agency; and the County of
Monroe, NY. Private funding sources include the Lannan Foundation for
support of the Lannan Translations Selection Series; the Max and Marian
Farash Charitable Foundation; the Mary S. Mulligan Charitable Trust; the
Rochester Area Community Foundation; the Steeple-Jack Fund; the Ames-
Amzalak Memorial Trust in memory of Henry Ames, Semon Amzalak, and Dan Amzalak;
and contributions from many individuals nationwide. See Colophon on page 104 for special
individual acknowledgments.

ART WORKS.
arts.gov

State of the Arts

NYSCA

Cover Design: Sandy Knight
Cover Art: Kai Carlson-Wee
Interior Design and Composition: Richard Foerster
Manufacturing: McNaughton & Gunn
BOA Logo: Mirko

Library of Congress Cataloging-in-Publication Data

Names: Carlson-Wee, Kai, author.
Title: Rail / by Kai Carlson-Wee.
Description: First edition. | Rochester, NY : BOA Editions, Ltd., 2018.
Identifiers: LCCN 2017044817 | ISBN 9781942683582 (softcover : acid-free paper)
Classification: LCC PS3603.A75345 A6 2018 | DDC 811/.6—dc23 LC record
available at https://lccn.loc.gov/2017044817

BOA Editions, Ltd.
250 North Goodman Street, Suite 306
Rochester, NY 14607
www.boaeditions.org
A. Poulin, Jr., Founder (1938–1996)

for Kristine Carlson and Morris Wee

CONTENTS

IV

V

FOREWORD

At times, poems can show us how to live, or at least point in the direction of what might be possible. How do we live in Kai Carlson-Wee's poems? We shoplift. We share. We skateboard. We skitch. We pass bottles of something back and forth, but do not drink from them—we inhale whatever it is that's inside. In "Dundas," a poem found near the end of this journey, the poet offers this: ". . . if God were enough, we keep / saying, but it's not . . ." Desperation drives many toward a low-level spirituality, yet here there is a refusal to accept easy consolation, especially in the unseen. We return to what can be slept upon— Rust. Lions. Trains. An old spirit named Cloudmaker is threaded throughout. Hobo, sage, trickster, he offers a way out. *This life*, he tells me, / *is one of those fake plastic rocks in the garden / you break with a hammer to get out / the key.*

The poems in *Rail* are inhabited by drifters, the generation that lingers in the downtowns of any American city, now with skateboards, now with earbuds, occasionally fucked up, hypervigilant to both beauty and danger, lost in an endless, epic, American nowhere. Here we are, riding the rails. Here we are, in train yards and hobo camps. Here we are, sensing, once again, how nothing can hold us, encountering, as Wallace Stevens wrote, the "Nothing that is not there and the nothing that is."

Like dark matter, that mysterious celestial substance, our speaker shimmers in the void, making a life for himself from little. Twenty-something, no parents in sight, no job, reeling from depression, he moves through the margins with only the myth of America and the stories of the past to guide him. There is a brother, but he is heartbroken. There are friends, but they are overdosing on heroin. There is a war, but it is the shadow of war. How do we come to terms with the epidemics of our culture? You won't find the answer here, just the effect, the husks, scattered across the heartland.

Everywhere we go in these poems we struggle to gather what's been left behind, what's been carried home. Home, though, is a complicated concept here. Here it is more a lack of anywhere to go, any alternative. This is a book steeped in location, but the location is diffuse. I wake somewhere on the outskirts of Portland. The cities in this book are the second cities . . . we aren't in Manhattan, we are in Fargo. We aren't in Los Angeles, we're in Flagstaff, places where "the killer was soon forgotten." In the poem "American Freight," which is epic, biblical, the poet offers this: "You forget your body / has form. Half in dream, half out." "American Freight" ends with the line, "It carries us home," but I sense it is, unlike for Ulysses, not from where he came. This home is something he has had to create, which is forever just beyond his grasp.

"Jesse James Days" is another watershed poem. It's a poem that seems to have come from somewhere outside of Carlson-Wee—I can imagine him staring at it, as I do, wondering at the old soul who created it. There is, again, that unsettling search for what is authentic, for what is a genuine feeling. "And what do we feel now, / watching the years float slowly by, as if in the skin / of another man?" This poem seems to capture that moment one turns briefly to look at oneself and finds someone unrecognizable: ". . . how we erase ourselves / knowingly, hands outstretched to the sound of it passing us, / letting the riders ride in." The ghosts of Frank Stanford, of Lynda Hull, of Sam Shepard, of Larry Levis haunt these poems, as well as something older. Maybe Woody Guthrie, maybe Walt Whitman (another war poet), if he hadn't found a spiritual home in the possibility of America. That possibility, that hope, may be long dead, but still there is something compelling here, something, as Whitman says, "with original energy."

Rust. Lions. Trains. This is the original energy that weaves throughout this fine, troubling, familiar book. Sketched out of dreams and quiet desperation, a search for the authentic banging against a sense of the forever receding past. *Rail* is timely, but also timeless. It shows us where we've been, but it also shows us where we might be going. If I were to put a book on a spaceship to show the aliens what it is like at this moment in America, this would be one of the books I'd choose. The aliens, though, would already know everything, they would see what is invisible and everywhere at once—in skateparks and alleyways, where poets and nomads, old and young, search ". . . for anything / other than home."

—Nick Flynn
October 2017

White freightliner,
won't you steal away my mind

—*Townes Van Zandt*

I dream of journeys repeatedly

—*Theodore Roethke*

RAIL

I find it here in the wild alfalfa, head full
of antipsychotics and blue rain. Twenty years old
on a freight train riding the soy fields
into the night. Leaning away from the shortgrass
prairie, the black Mississippi of dream.
My brother asleep on the well-wall beside me,
nodding his head to the sway. What home
are we leaving? What distances blur
the electric fence? What hundred low thundering
wheels of darkness are coming to carry us
there? Rain and the singing wind, over
the auto-racks. Staring out west at the stars
of our gods and the lonely dark stars of our hearts.
Boarded-up storefronts, burned-down
apartments, highway signs that only name
the dead. We cross the station tracks,
the broken legs of Sunday chairs left rusting
in the yards. We know the way the story ends.
Still, the whistle blows. The flare stacks whip
their excess methane candles against
the night. The wheels that brought us this far
still roll, still churn the polished iron ash.
The road goes on. The highway turns a deeper
shade of black. And as the sun sinks down
on the eastern Montana hills, peppered with horses
and gun-shot cars, the rails still lead us
somewhere else, and shine in the falling light.

THRESHER

There has to be a tree. There has to be
a sky. There has to be a chicken hawk
skating the dust rising out of a thresher.
A plow boy walking with a turtle
in the head-high corn. There has to be a pool
with a swirly slide entering the water.
A chain-link cut by the field where I took
Kerri-Ann to the river when the river
was flooded. A burnt knife lettering
her knee. And a song being played—
All the girls are gone, All the headstrong
good country girls are gone—from the window
of a painted Accord. Her father standing drunk
in the screen porch watching us dance.
There has to be light falling into his body.
And a muskie we pull from the mud puddles
under the tracks. A reason we throw it
in the pool where it wobbles and floats
in the shivering wave-lines. Her father still
watching us dance in his sleep. There has to be
a fight, a crossfade of landscape surrounding
those liquor-marked breaths. Him catching
her thigh. The two of them wishing to God
they were drunker. And the black lines
of telephone wires rise quiet as old men
or grocery store crosses. The scarecrow
in silhouette losing its face in the hyper-
colored dust and the clouds. There has to be
light. And a circling car. And a song
moving out of his body like something
he names. A chicken hawk rising
on dust trails over the ditch where the boy
now plays. The river still flooded.
The dissipated clouds in late-day in awe
of their own color fading. There has to be

a flood. And a promise of love. And a fish
in the pool, and the pool gone dark
where the turtle glides under the leaves.

SUNSHINE LIQUIDATORS

Biking through downtown Bellingham,
nothing but partyboys staggering back
to their cars in the dark, the sound
of a distant muffler, the hum of a vent
where the bakers are kneading the bread,
we stop at the Sunshine Liquidators,
opening bag after bag of garbage,
hoping for bread or chips or eggs
or cartons of soy milk, one day expired.
My brother moves quietly over his
headlamp, handing me overripe plantains
and mangoes, Hass avocados from San Joaquin,
spoiled and black in my hands. *Maybe
there's something to save here*, he says,
passing a flat sack of carrot cake muffins,
a Styrofoam package of trout. Above us
the motion-light glosses a window,
bending our shadows against the far wall,
kinking our heads at the hard angles.

DEPRESSION

after Robert Bly

I felt the roof of my head break and clatter
to the floor. I felt the particles dance
in the empty and electric air, turning around in circles
like plastic bags caught in a draft.
I thought the river would swallow me whole,
and the seagulls would never stop sailing away.
Now the deer bones rattle on the bare wall.
Night winds rest and clouds
advance on clouds. Days fall back
inside themselves like water.
Now the river takes its color from the weeds
and my friends are half asleep
in their anticipated lives, dreaming in the vain styles
of their age, painting their childhoods
over their eyes, walking the ribbons
of highways like crows. Now my mind
moves back to my father's Easter sermon,
walking alone in the dark garden,
lighting the trashcans on Division Street
on fire, watching the fat police lumber
to the flames. And my thirteenth birthday,
setting off flares in the train yard, scraping my name
on the rust-lined door. What became
of those abbreviated years? Now they slump
inside these littered banks of sand.
Now my face is hard to look at
when I sleep. The words become like putty
in my ear. Now the cold hours wake me
in the night, the oak leaves fall and linger in the wind,
the swallows leave the shadow for the bridge
and the carp float dead in the metal grates below.

THE FOG AND THE SOUND

Volunteers in kayaks and other small boats searched Saturday, June 6th, for two men who have been missing since their sailboat capsized near Chuckanut Bay. Friends gathered where the sailboat washed ashore south of Post Point, breaking the boat apart with an electric saw and a sledgehammer.

—*Bellingham Herald, June 7th, 2009*

My brother lived with a girl named Grace, until Grace broke his heart and rode Greyhound nine hundred miles to live with a dancer in San Joaquin. There was no explanation, he said. Just a few weird months and the ocean in back of their house still rolling the fog off Chuckanut Bay.

In early May the two of us walked down the railroad tracks toward the nude beach, stopping to spraypaint our names on the outcropping rocks, the anonymous driftlogs, the sweating cathedral-like slabs of cement near the train tunnel entrance, which no one could see.

A storm had just passed and the Jet Skiers cruised through the inlets and low tide estuaries looking for Gunther, a snowboarder left by his friends in the capsized shell of his grandfather's yacht. The front end sank. The sail fell down so the motor blades cried in the wind.

He said he had loved her forever. The time in the mountains, the time in the Red Canyon pledging their lives. The loss of her touch, he told me, was not the loss of her callused hands, her body's weight rolling against him in bed. It was the loss of a thing he had loved in himself, as he turned his head hearing her voice. *Do you know what I mean*, he said, *that difference?*

On Monday we went to the blood bank with Duncan and looked at the holes in the ceiling expand. The pattern of checkerboard squares in the bathroom, the sad diabetic man turning away from the desk, going back to his truck, getting in. For an hour the blood moved in clear plastic hoses between us.

The Cloudmaker showed us the scars on his arms where the cops pulled the real bones out of him. Surgically opened his forehead. Fixed him with circuits and gold-plated grommets designed to control him and steal his dreams. *Smells like a woman's arousal*, he said, *the weather itself is a burden of shame, the dust in my pocket, the atmosphere bleeding.*

We skated downtown with the rat-tailed hipsters who showed us the dumpster behind the museum. Sallow-eyed, practicing shiftys. We skitched on the door of a broken Mercedes. We shouldered them over the barbwire fences and jumped off the guardrails into the sea.

The fog seemed to thicken our bodies the way it divided the ground from the trees. Fattening up our hair, blowing the sweat trails out of our jeans. Wavering gulls in the airwaves above their own shadows. A dusting of salt we could taste on our skin.

He showed me the painting she painted him in. The pallet of blues and raw umbers she used for the pavement, the signpost, the bike he had just finished riding from Portland to Havre, from Havre to Nashville, from Nashville to Kitty Hawk, North Carolina to sleep in the wind-torn dunes.

We stayed awake talking of winters in Fargo, the riverside houses condemned or abandoned, a mutual friend who had recently died. I tried to remember the last time I saw him, placid from heroin, walking the bar with the overheads glossing the flat-looking bowls of his eyes.

On Friday we went to the food shelf and stood with the homeless and gutter-punks feeding their dogs. How many, they asked us. We filled up our boxes. The Mexicans shuffled their children in silence. The Cloudmaker juggled his oranges and sang us the ballad he knew by heart.

There were pockets of sandstone carved by the high-tide waves where the girls would take off their clothes and dissolve in the sun or watch freightliners crawl through the haze. A wake-line dividing the shore from the shore. A dander of lotion I peeled away from the stone.

The morning they found him we walked down the railroad tracks toward the shipyard, stopping to throw a few rocks at the mile signs, tossing the starfish from pool to pool. His body was found in a box trap, bloated and skin-torn by schools of minnows, eyes eaten out of his head by the crabs.

It wasn't the fact of her leaving. The winter he spent with a sprained ankle, limping. The spear-point of rebar she pulled from his hand after bailing a still-moving train. It was more like the fog, he said. Like fields in winter, dust in the air when the street sweepers watered the roads.

Before I drove back to Seattle we hiked up Mount Fernow, carrying our sleeping bags under our arms. We sat on the roots of a dead ponderosa and looked at the ships troll the narrows in fog. There were lights on the city shore shining and burning. Beach fires fading and pushing like strobes.

When lightning came over the harbor we stood at the back of his house and rolled smokes. We counted the seconds, predicted the levels of thunder. For a while we lay with our elbows just touching. The blown away screens. The sound of the wind and the rain coming down on the roof.

OAKS

Nights like these where the road empties out
around ten, goes dead, leaves only distances.
Here to the stop sign, the telephone pole,
the streetlight pooling at the intersection.
Sometimes the drone of quiet machines
in the back alley next to my house.
Feeling the spring air crawl through the matted-down
grass, crusty with trash melted out of the snow.
The moon takes its time with whatever it does,
disappears mostly. Tries not to draw
much attention to itself. The way
I return to the same place repeatedly,
working the insignificant details.
Naked in the dark room. Feeling around
for the sides of your breasts, the knob
of your shoulder, coiling back,
pumping your collarbone against me.
In my mind's eye the trail of your vertebrae
descends forever. One socket holding
the next one in place. Fence line. Wavering
leaves on the stand-alone oak trees, shyly alive
in the night wind. From the top of the hill
I see floodlights on the ballfield below me,
looking like a party I just missed out on.
Something tremendous the crowd left abandoned
and wandered away from toward nothing particular,
hoping for some other miracle.

MENTAL HEALTH

One pill in the morning with breakfast. Orange juice
and oatmeal. Brown sugar melted on top. No coffee.
No cigarettes. One multivitamin with extra niacin for
stress relief, natural. One St. John's Wort and a dab
of Valerian Root extract under the tongue. Hold it
for ten seconds and swallow it down. Leave the house
in the rhythmic rain. Two blocks waiting for the city
bus under the awning of M & H Gas. Two-dollar fare
for the next four hours. The crowded seats and broken
black umbrellas against the edge. You can ride all day
if you know the right driver. Half an Ativan under
the tongue for stress relief. Hold it until it dissolves.
Chew the powder from molar to molar. Swallow
the excess down. Ride the rain-soaked streets of fog.
The rising fog and drifting fog that slithers on the lake.
The parking lot fog and cemetery headstones, branches
of maples and swerving commuter cars finding their way
to the fastest lane. The folding doors open and people
continue to climb the lighted stairs. Stop after stop
and the plastic goulashes and shopping bags dripping
with rain. The man behind you selling a rock of crack
to a younger man, homeless. They shake the plastic
bag and all goes on again, normal, with real affection.
Weather and breakfast and Halloween costumes and
where the bus might stop next. Open your backpack
and take out a racquetball. Squeeze it between your
thighs and remember to count your breaths. Think of
your favorite places to hike. The mountains extending
beyond you forever in four different fields of cloud.
Decide to get off the bus and walk. The driver nods
and rain beats down and the uptown businessmen
shuffle beneath the bulbous roof of glass. All your steps
are washed away in the smallest shining flood. Walk
the blocks and count the squares and count the endless
passing cars. The lights are red and liquid gold and fog

continues to touch your legs and search for a way inside
your brain. Your ears, your open mouth, your nose.
It moves itself toward every hole. Open your backpack
and take out a Seroquel, morning and night, for distorted
thoughts and hallucinations. Hold the taste against your
tongue and count your breaths and close your eyes
and remember to watch the graceful gait of mule deer
crossing the ridge. Barely a year old, lonely together,
they move through paintbrush and dew-soaked heather
and alder and aspen and down through larches and gold-
tinted boulders to drink from Railroad Creek. You watch
the cars divide the fog. Water rolls between the lanes.
You cross the Kmart parking lot, the Lake Street bridge
and drowning lights. You count the weight of every
breath. You know it can't go on like this. But here you
are. This is life. This is the way your day begins.

FREDDY KRUEGER

Fuck this rain, man. You want a smoke?
Here, take one. At least it fills you up with
something. Gives you some heat. I'd give
you the shirt off my back if you needed.
I'd buy you a house if I won the prize. I'm
a generous man underneath it. For real,
I was bullied by this guy once. I let him in
my apartment. He said he was a friend,
an acquaintance. He took my body apart.
Fucked up my room real good. Broke
all my shit, shattered my glass plates. Now
I walk with this gimpy leg. I know I look
homeless. I know I look like a weirdo to
people. I've got this shoulder blade thing.
I can't feel my face on the right side. It's
useless to try and press charges. It's just
Freddy Krueger, man. It's some kind of
nightmare I can't get away from. I've been
punching air, I've just been swinging. It's
like I'm not even here. These citizens
look right through me. They walk and
keep walking. I could have been a real
person. I could have changed my life.
I'm not retarded. I know what I see when
I look in the mirror. I met the devil, man.
Straight up. He said he was looking to
buy some weed. Hang out. I used to do
music. I used to have a hip-hop thing in
Detroit. This was back in the day. Like
1996. We used to do shows. We used to
play skateparks and run-down houses,
anyone's party. I heard him knock and I
opened the door. He broke me in half,
took all my records and shit, my widescreen
TV. He did what he wanted. The floor

of my room started shining. It looked like
a layer of stars. Like a hole made of liquid
glass. Sometimes at night there's a shine
over there on the street. I can see it from
my window. Right under the taco stand.
It's safe over there when the shine comes
down. At least then I know I'm not dreaming.

KING

for Nik Zeidlhack 1981–2007

I go to the guardrail, looking out over the sea-foam.
Looking out over the salmon heads breaking
the waves. Muscling back to the place of their birth.
Trapped in the floodlights, failing to leap up the dam.
Sometimes the clarity. Sometimes the clarity
and night-river steaming. Time standing still
in its permanent memory. Flies in the backwater
gathered to feed on the skin. The smell of the ocean.
The waters combining with other more powerful
waters. Riding away from whatever would save them,
knowing the other direction is pointless and not worth
suffering through. What holds us together but also
what trembles. The first time you look at an actual lion,
pacing the length of its cage. The small irreversible
ink-stain breaking the face of whatever we skate on.
Slumped at the edge of your girlfriend's bed. Your
pulse gone flat. No sweat. No resistance. No steam
on the hand-held mirror they tested for breath.
The day you were found I watched ducks drop down
on the Nooksack River in pairs. Drifting together
in multicolored light, leaving small growing trails
behind them. At first I thought only the lights
were alive. The river, the fish, the clusters of flies—
they were tricks being played on the eyes. But now,
getting up on the guardrail, watching the line
where the river and ocean waves meet, the half-formed
outriders failing inside us, and something behind
all the highway signs shining. Not clarity of thought,
or light, or time. But clarity of small things believing
in themselves. Dark heads breaking the surface
again. More than the living. More than the dead.

WHERE THE FEELING DESERTS US

I wake somewhere on the outskirts of Portland.
The crickets are singing. The train is refusing
to breathe. Off in the distance a truck gears down
on a service road bordered in trees. The river
beside me, babbling kind. Headache. Earache.
All I can see of the field dissolves in a stale white blanket
of moon. Nothing moves. Even the cold machinery
seems to be riding itself in a dream.
Sliding away from the steel retainer walls.
Boxcars stalled on the next four strings. The train
is my shepherd. I finger a dead leaf. Star-lights dance
in the field beyond my cage. We are never returning
to the field itself, only the mystery hidden inside.
Night after night in the speed of your leaving.
Soft of your veined hands tracing my thigh.
The flavor of dust where the feeling deserts us.
Maybe the blond heads of needlegrass swaying.
Bodies of cows in the next field over. I pull up the blanket
to cover my bare arms. Cool air filled
with the pressures of falling dew. This is the best
I can give for a reason—the metal accepts you,
whoever you are. The train you are riding will only
go forward. The straight line is perfectly clear.

AFTER HAVRE

> In his alleged confession, Hickman says he cut up the body with intentions
> of disposing of it, but later realized that he could not obtain the $1,500
> unless he presented the girl to the father, whereupon he reconstructed
> the body as best he could to make it appear that Marian was still alive.
> —*Havre Daily News, December 26, 1927*

Waiting forever in the damp night—
burnt-orange skeletal overheads galvanizing the rails
in the black space behind us. Montana,
west side of Havre, stalled in a crap town,
waiting for the coal bucks a half-mile up to get filled.
Bulls in the jungle like janitors cleaning the sinks,
flashing a light now and then, sympathetic.
I can tell you the wheels in my ears
will not give. Not for the next few days.
I can tell you the crust punk who waded through soy fields
in Fargo, eye-stabbed with an old pair of scissors,
one dog after him. Childhood birthdays
I can't seem to access. Parked in the brain
with invisible cities. Trials of proving ourselves
more alive—I don't understand where it leaves us.
Lost in the tar grease and prairie dust
laced on the wasted Dakotas; what do we do
with a regular dream? Red Cloud. Geronimo.
Casey Jones chasing the million seasons of Dylan.
Heywood refusing to open the safe. Hickman arranging,
then rearranging the body. Cruising along
through another comparable nightmare.
Comfortable somehow, resigned to the fact
of illegally ducking for three days, catching
the full-faced whiff of insecticide sprinklers,
fields of junked cars and ramblers, fence lines
with plastic bags flaming the wind.
You can feel it going before it goes.
Shivers along the connections, revived

by the engines. Five of them, suddenly pressing
their weight to the backline. Cracking along
the imaginary spine as my own bucket lurches,
and rattles toward Portland.

POET AT TWENTY-FOUR

In those days the wind seemed to whittle me down
to the root. Round off my fingers as if I were some
piece of glass in the evening sea. If you saw me
at the grocery store picking through fruit,
my backpack hanging behind,
eyes gone slack as a turned-off TV at the Radio Shack
in the mall, testing the peaches and ripe avocados,
scratching the skin of a grapefruit
for luck, you would barely have noticed
the hawk's foot necklace I wore on a copper
electrical wire, the ribbon of foil I glued to my beanie
to block out invisible low-wave rays.
If you saw me at a coffee shop watching the crowd,
scribbling notes on a wrinkled receipt,
you would never have noticed yourself in those words,
but you would be there still,
in the softest rhyme, in streetlight spilling across
your empty cup. You would be the simple
wish of mist, the unnameable music that kept me alive,
even after you turned to forget who I was
and left through the automatic doors.

MISS DIANA

I wasn't always this way. I was raised in a house
of religion. My parents were lovely and kindhearted
people. They treated me fine. Just fine. Whatever
I wanted to play with was mine. I ran in the backyard
naked. I danced at the Veteran's Hall on the weekend.
Sang in the choir. I never did anything wrong. I rode my
chestnut horse in the sun. My dad called him *Sweetness*.
He lived for the prairie. For the big country sun
in his face. The sun has its favors to give. It *rejoices*.
People say, Miss Diana, why do you always sit
in the sun? Why don't you sit over there in the shade?
Why don't you sleep in the shelter with friends?
Those people don't understand *freedom*. They take off
their clothes in the bathroom at night. They are
serious fuckers. They would burn down the house
with a single lit match. A single lit match and the whole
hotel would be gone. They would poison the well
with a drop of blood. With a Red Bull. I am pretty much
hateful of Red Bull. I lived with a man once. He would
always drink Red Bull. Morning, afternoon, evening, night.
He was addicted to methamphetamine. Speed. It was
the worst four years of my life. He kept me in bondage.
In psychological fear. The light changed only inside
the house. The windows all blacked out. Music playing
loudly. I was a *hostage*. I was a kidnapping victim
of *choice*. An adult kidnapping victim. I write the words
on my hand to remember. I write the words on my shoe
so the road will remember my name. I was here.
I existed alone in these streets. My name is Diana
and I was born free and I am not his anymore to possess.

THE BOY'S HEAD

after Roberto Bolaño

There was a year or two when none of it mattered. I woke up late, sat on the balcony porch with a cigarette, turned on the gas-light to scramble some eggs. Days seemed to flash and fold away like pages in a magazine. No one knew my name, and if they did, they didn't bring me up in conversation. I was living off the grid, in the gaudy retirement halls of the Mount Helix Apartments. My hair fell down in complete abandon, swinging from eye to eye. Usually tied in the back with rubber bands, or with shoelaces somebody left on the curb. Nobody cared about my style. On weekends I went to the skatepark in El Cajon and attempted to flirt with the girls. People came through, disappeared, made claims. The sun never altered its place in the sky. The floodlights came on and the metalheads listened to boomboxes perched on the stairs. I was down there one day in September, a day like any other day, when a boy's head was found in the playing field, cut with a hacksaw, circled in little white stones. Local authorities said it was a "gang thing" or a "satanic ritual kind of thing." They said it was a product of organized crime, an "underground collective," although no one really knew. The troubling part, to me at least, was that the boy wasn't even from town—he was on vacation with his parents from North Dakota, traveling by motorhome, headed for Zion and Flagstaff, Mount St. Helens, Vancouver, Rainier. For the first few days there was vague speculation, but no one came forward and no one was blamed. Weeks later, it seemed as though nothing had happened. The park flags waved in the same lacking breezes, the tennis balls hung in the chain-link fence, the skaters continued to circle the bowl, and the killer was soon forgotten.

THE CLOUDMAKER'S BAG

He shows me the camp stove he cooks with.
Ten-dollar poker chips. Crystals he carries
in small leather pouches, tied to his shoelace,
his belt loops to harness the sun. He carries
a matchbook, a cell phone and charger, a lighter,
an old deck of playing cards with nudes
on the backs of them, needles and balled thread,
thin strips of tinfoil wrapped up in two yellow
Ziploc bags. He carries his own wife's bones
on a necklace. Fingers them round in the glow
of the shelter lights. Nuggets he dug from
the cremator's shoebox of ash. He is seven
years homeless now. Living on handouts,
gravedigger jobs he has only been fired from,
free meals down at the church. He carries
a homemade knife in his pocket. Dull gray.
Whetstone for keeping the blade-tip able
to break through aluminum cans. Watermark
stains on the handle from leaving it drawn
in the seaside rain. He carries a King James.
He carries a loose gold tooth on a string. He
carries a phony ID in his wallet. Stranger from
Delaware, barely resembles him. Writes
down the names of the good eucalyptus trees.
Calls them his *Darlings*, his *Leafy-green Loves*.
He carries an old pair of foggy binoculars,
out-of-date passport, a penlight for writing his words
on the night sky. Something he picked up in Bozeman,
Montana. *The stars are so clear there, they beg*
for connections. For someone to map out
their infinite faces. To draw the invisible lines.

THE BOOK

I went to a place where the wind had died, where the sun was resting its heaviest light on the clouds, where the water was perfect and looked like glass. What was the point of forgiveness again? That year of forgetting your face. The snow came down. The speedboats covered themselves in tarps, engine oil drained. The eagle I knew stood perfectly still in the crown of a Norway pine. I stayed for months, watching birds. Seasons changed. Women came and went, leaving clothes, antique rings, cigarette butts in the cans. I woke at night to the sound of wolves, shivering in my chair. I kept a knife beneath the bed. Once a week I went for food, beer and bottled water for my hair. I called my mom. I knew the couple down the road—Rosie and Ray Albers. They loaned me books and DVDs, dropped me off a hotdish now and then. I learned to walk away from words. At night I burned the candles in the glass. Flame to flame. Shadows crawling softly through the woods. I saw a falcon kill a robin in the spring. Took it straight out of the air. Put a talon through its throat and flew away. I don't know why I stayed so long. I stayed until I wrote the book. I stayed until your face became the lake, the snowy roads, the birds.

FLY FISHING

And the cutting and stripping the guts out.
Taking the knife behind the gills. Holding the tail
against the grass. Is there no understanding the secret of death
in the dying? We see the fear come up in the eyes,
the final incredible kick, the heart valve opened
as wide as it goes. The slow release
lasting longer than we thought possible—
the tail still flapping, the severed head
still sucking a long useless O
from the air. The small fin flattens
in my hand. The smallest heart I have ever seen,
there in the neck hole, still beating.
Eyes gone slack, somehow more open.
And the fact of death goes sliding out
on the perfect glass of the lake. Pale and gold
in the cloud-light, tossing a spark on the mayflies'
wings. They hover together, riding the dock ends,
descending on the dark water to feed.

JESSE JAMES DAYS

If I called to you now. If I carried your name to the skateparks
and railroad temples of rust, would you come to me, brother,
wherever you are in your faded arrangements,
your growing away from the past? Would you lie with me here
in the shore grass, watching the college boys paint
the gazebo, the endless advance and retreat of the sea?
I'm trying to imagine us back to our origins.
Skitching the Friday night dump truck in Moorhead,
shoplifting soft packs of Camel Lights,
kicking our boards through the rodeo crowds at the fair,
searching the beer tent for half-finished bottles of High Life,
for cigarette butts in the ashtrays, for lighters,
for dime bags and dollar bills left on the tables, for anything
other than home. We were saved from oblivion once.
Slack in the shoulder blades. Climbing the roofs
of the for-sale houses in Dundas, diving off chimney tops,
ladder rungs, letting our bodies go limp in the arms
of the pines. And here on the fog-covered beach in Bolinas
a girl is rolling her jeans up, gathering seashells and green-tinted nuggets
of sea glass, letting the high water circle
her knees. I watch her approach in the rippled light, lifting a sand dollar,
lost in the sound. I can almost see light falling out
of her body, the space where the sea wind is too shy
to touch her, too embarrassed to run itself
under her shirt. What grainy, impossible dreams
used to guide us? What wildernesses burned on the vacated stages
and bankrupt resorts of our brains?
Anders, we get old. We divide ourselves up into seasons,
digressions, failed attractions, glorified versions
of jaded and lost men we promised
to never become. Do you remember the Indian
selling us dusters and turtle skulls under the bridge?
And watching the staged reenactment at sunset, the overgroomed horses
and amplified pleadings of Heywood refusing
to open the safe. Refusing to hear what it meant

they would do to him—carving an X in his collarbone,
cracking his skull with the butt of a gun.
The teller lying dead in a puddle of blood
beside him. The sound of the bullet that ripped off his ear,
more a physical weight than a sound, a texture of things
growing suddenly far away, fattening, filled with a needling buzz.
The ease with which he could picture those three
silent numbers, floating like neon-lit billboards against
the darkening lids of his eyes. Really just simple
abstractions, marks on a chalkboard, lines in a ledger that nobody else,
besides himself and the wealthy proprietor
who sometimes stopped in on Sundays
with his twin boys to look at the weekly reports,
could read. Do you remember the way the horses were trained
to carefully lower their heads, to give us the softest part of their jaws,
regardless of whether we carefully touched them
or offered them handfuls of grain? And do you remember
the way we discovered the Indian,
slumped in the willow reeds, dotted with secondhand light
from the Tilt-A-Whirl sign, sniffing a milk gallon,
laughing at shapes in the overhung ceiling of leaves?
How we were able to recognize the irony,
even then. And even more than the irony, the inevitability
of all things defined by their pasts, by duties that outlive
the vanishing crowds, their instruments measuring
dust. And how you approached him again
as a stranger, and sat at the base of the willow tree,
pressing your nose to the outheld mouth of the jug.
And the river crawled off in a fever of lights
and the music was suddenly clear. Anders, come rest with me here
in the shore grass, leaning away from the wind.
Enough of these shivers and tentative symbols,
these crab shells and wind-whitened rails
of sand. I want you to walk with this young girl
in silence, speak to her only in footprints, in subtler signs
she can read in the foam, explain to her how we erase ourselves
knowingly, hands outstretched to the sound of it passing us,
letting the riders ride in. The way you became

this ridiculous whisper, sky growing vague in a cover of fog—
whatever description, assemblage of passages,
memories left to the dead. And what do we feel now,
watching the years float slowly by, as if in the skin
of another man? What do we find in the comfort
of time's absent shadow? Shooting our guns
at the city-born crows. Chucking our bricks at the immigrant carp
in the backwater next to the dam. Look, we are losing ourselves
to the waves. Faltering after it. Claiming or trying to reclaim
the inventions. Wishing for, naming the magic away.
Tell me, what fissures, what twinkling dimples of light
came spiraling out of your face? As the cries
of the fairgoers danced on the water,
and the actor who played Jesse James for the weekend
went down to the beer tent, took off his holster,
his button-up chaps, his handgun that only
shot blanks, and danced to the fiddle and lap steel guitar,
to the rhythmless crowd, and the hollowed-out sound of the bullet
that still seemed to ring in the streets, that will ring there forever,
in the unopened vault, in the scattered remains of an ear.

BOLINAS

Memory treats us unfairly at first,
revealing only the clouds and rust,
the feeling of welding-dust blowing
against our lips. Only later do we see
the invisible robin she carried inside
her chest, the sense of its wet weight
stranded in her hands, the silence
and subtle change of heart that filled
the room. Only later do we see how
the bitterness grew in the stomach,
filtered its way to the shoulders and
ribs, the lower extremities, crown
of the head. You can feel it pushing
its way to the roof cracks, searching
the windows and slats in the blinds,
the down-hanging pink strands of old
insulation. Only later, two or three
years now, walking alone on the fog-
covered beach in Bolinas, smoking
alone at the back of the garage,
do you see that the tear in her eye
that one night, watching her come
in the moonlit boat, was not for your
beauty, not for a shared sense of wind
on the body, but for some other man
she had failed to name. A man she
had loved for his strangeness and anarchy,
free methamphetamine, shaky tattoos.
A man she would never have stayed with
or married, but who she loved beyond
reason, and lost track of long ago.

STEAMPIPE

The trick is to boil the water, he says,
*then carefully drop the nugget of glass
inside*. He shivers his fingers to show
the resulting steam, which will spread out thinly,
rising above his enormous head, perfectly
odorless, barely a mist in the late-day sun.
Another man walks from the camp at the riverbank,
rolling the end of his shirt like a sack.
I got one here, he says, *seined us a toad*.
He holds up a little black tadpole,
kicking its one black leg in the air.
Put it in the bowl, the first man says,
and positions the lighter beneath
the pipe. They watch it circle the tiny bulb
of light. Eyelessly searching the edge,
hooking and cracking its leg like a whip.
The water begins to bubble and drift,
swirl in colorless patterns of heat.
The one man laughs as the first man takes
a hit, and the spinning body, writhing now,
knocking its head against the glass,
begins to glow.

CRYSTAL METH

for Kerri-Ann

We are held in a light so perfect it grows inconsistent.
Becomes like the windwheel cries on the prairie.
Tags on the wall of a townhouse garage you can barely
make out from a train. Do you remember the looming
cathedral of cloud? Standing in the driveway of your
father's house, wiping your nose, saying beauty was
more like the heart of a rock, like paintings of ducks
at the swapmeet tent, or the curve of the cul-de-sac
swallowed in corn. A sudden demand to acknowledge
the concrete, flea market gnomes in the garden,
the ground. The lion being real for the first time,
maybe. The winter consistency made more clear.
You could see it as dream, or you could see it
as dreaming. A cat's other eye, or a dog's wild kicking
at night. And the truth is we don't have a choice
which it is—our thoughts only travel so far. If God
were enough, or the layers of crust in a pen-cap pipe.
The moon only pushes us farther apart—the drive-in
abandoned, billboards grafittied in blue rust,
the body resigning itself by the year. Returning again
to the trampoline later that night, fingering blade after
blade of grass, examining each little kink in each
thin root, making me promise, making me swear
to kill you, to physically jam a knife in your throat
if you ever did this again. But walking my fingers
across your back, your flattered cheeks, your effortless,
practiced charms, the wet sheet hugging your flattened
breasts, floating like two wide lilies from one side
of your chest to the other, as if you were a secret body
of water, flooded with catfish and half-buried tires—
I know we can never deny this weakness. Never ignore
this chemical standard we'll never be able to touch.
Because love is a field we measure between us. Songs

of our breathing. A tower of light we keep chasing away
from a cloud. And we ruin this beauty by calling it
substance, innocence, wilderness, babyface, girl.

WALLS OF THE JUNGLE

Goldie / Shenanigans / Red River Drifter Crew / Do without duties / Invisible Riders Crew / Last one to Stupidsville / Answer Plus Question Mark / Got fucked in Jungletown / Lefty and Lefty's dog / Heads up and heads down / Smells like an anarchist / Old Boy Will Kill You For Oxy, Don't Trust Him! / Bulls check the fences at sunset and midnight / Fuck all inventions / The Gods might be communists / Angel-eyes / Spider Eyes / Ezra will pound you down / Outbound to SF with Dayglo and Baby Jane / Guts and Dust / Gutter's groove / Twiggie's Old Dominion Crew / No one here gets out alive / Bound for Texas / Dye your eyes / Hear that lonesome whistle blow / Chance and Grace in '96 / Half these kids are fucking grommets / All aboard the westbound train / Who the hell is Seventh Sea? / Done with Northtown, Sims got busted / Going driftless / Leave Me B / Oh, sweet momma, take me home / Where the weather suits my clothes / Where the chilly winds don't blow / Lord, I'm going down that road

III

AMERICAN FREIGHT

Under the bridge in the Midtown Yard
where I slept three nights and eventually caught my train,
you can read the graffiti of all the itinerant hobos
who hunkered there, out of the rain,
smoking their filters and waiting for rides
in the north Minneapolis night.
You can read their names: Spider Eyes, Doorknob, Stitch,
in the faint black lines
of a permanent marker the pigeon shit slowly erodes.
Bedrolls and cardboard boxes for mattresses,
half-gallon bottles of Schnapps.
If you look hard enough
you can make out the poem I carved in the truss overhead,
left there to fade with drippings
and winter exhaust turning everything slowly to rust:
I dream of journeys repeatedly. Westbound to Seatown. 2010.

❖❖❖

Moving now. Under the tower light dropping industrial glow
on my head. River beside me,
swallowing all of it, blending the real invisible stars
with the red-blinking light of the FRED.
Stone Arch Bridge and the Metrodome rooftop.
Gold Medal Mill sign flickering orange, on and off,
and beyond it the high glass hospital walls
where my mother looked down at the wide Mississippi
and sang to her firstborn son. Held me up
jaundiced and covered in dew,
my lungs just beginning to wheeze.
It is all there. High in those floating glass squares
where the sick are being treated and privately
dying, and the mothers are waiting

and new fathers waiting and wandering down
to the vending machines where the windows look out
at the factory stacks
and the big muddy river of iron and blood
where my train disappears in the night.

❖❖❖

The antipsychotics I took that year made the world
inside me sublime. My eyes moved over the shape of a face,
the delicate wind in a tree.
I felt nothing. I wrote no poems.
The language of beauty divided itself into basic descriptions
of fact. I wandered from place to place,
stoplight to stoplight,
waiting for something to break from the skyline,
force me to finally stay.
I gained weight. I measured my sadness in lies.
In small medications. Doses.
I smelled things that couldn't be there,
convinced I was dying from an airborne chemical
someone had blown in my ear.
But then there were moments of pure
unexplainable light. Clouds held signs
in their elegant swells. You could feel them rubbing
their moonlit backs on the fields
of darkness behind. Sometimes I noticed a face in the glass,
in the polished aluminum wall of a downtown bank,
and for a moment of sweetness
I knew I was gone. I was nothing to speak of,
no one at all. And the stranger I saw
looking back in the dark
was a man with no future, no name to remember,
no place in the world but this.

❖❖❖

Over the clay dirt. Over the fields of unthreshed wheat,
the sun-white skulls in the railroad ditch. Over the rattling
weight of this train. The silos in Dilworth. The Williston
oil rigs fracking the unmarked Chippewa graves. Over
the lonely cry, lost now. Miles of dark stars, dirt roads
leading in every direction away from whatever you are.
Midtown to Mandan. Dilworth to Butte. Highballing
west on a wheel of sun dogs, prayers, and no goodbyes.

❖❖❖

Who are you? Stranger who gave me the last of your
laughter. Waited all night
for the Eastbound departure, your Rottweiler guarding
the dark. Rolling your cigarettes one-handed,
knowing the story is always the same,
no matter how far you are
from home. Traveling poet,
songwriter busking for leftover pizza and posting your lines
to a blog. Your history made up and sketchy
at best. Your lovely, obedient dog.
I fed her granola bars out of my backpack,
made sure the water stayed full. The moonlight ignoring
your tattooed face, the skeleton hand on your neck.
We are shadows now,
born to the shape of departure. The engine
a feverish bird underneath me. Wingbeats. Gathering speed.

❖❖❖

Storm clouds again outside Fargo,
again outside Glasgow. Now trailing off into thunderheads breaking
in great gray flowers above the road.
Flecks of blue. Passionate rain in the underswells.
Minor flirtations of sun.
Man covered head-to-toe in oil outside Williston.
Unreal.
Flares in the distance and windwheels
carving the sky.
Decapitated dog on the ballast rock. Still wet.
Chest flashing under the train-line shadow
and seeming to secretly breathe.
Somewhere in the distance a lazy alarm sounds off
in a four-four beat. Bull frogs sing as if trying
to return the call.
Tricoloreds fly and the slow sashay of cottonwood branches above.
The day is born with each new feather,
each fern leaf bending to touch the ground.
Each minor vibration. Each river of heaven
I lower myself in to drink.

❖❖❖

The Cloudmaker tells me the name of the train,
the number of engines to look for,
the exact bush to bury myself in shade.
You know by the speed and direction it exits,
the number of minutes it waits.
Orange hats for yard workers, Oakleys for bulls—
you can look at the bones of those old prehistorics.
Suicide buckets and gold forty-eights.
You can find it by watching the axle-bolts turn.
Soo Line. Norfolk. Union Pacific. Amtrak. CSX.
Kansas & Western. Burlington Northern Santa Fe.

❖❖❖

Are all roads endless? Do all roads blend
into one wide road, which ends in a field of unmowed grass
and returns to itself forever?
The Cloudmaker stands on a corner in Minot,
talking a prayer to himself and the rain.
The Cloudmaker rides out of Staples and Whitefish,
filling his bag from a dumpster at Walgreens,
watching the traffic lights
turning for blind cows—crickets in Dunsmuir, ducks in the dreamery,
plastic-wrapped chickens in grocery store aisles
and thresher dust bleaching
the stars. The wayward Canada geese.
The painted facades of train station depots, murals
of Crazyhorse, shit-stained pewter of dead or dying soldiers
clutching their bodies in Custer,
oxidizing softly, deeper
and deeper green,
climbing a hill in their permanent imaginations—
grassfires, vast plains, fields of buffalo thundering under the ground.

❖❖❖

We enter the storm. Cattlebirds calling out, thunderheads
bleeding a thin green light on the corn.
Feeling of rain and then rain itself,
streaking the railroad dust on my arm.
Lightning breaks out.
I let rain fall into my open mouth, fill it up, tasting
the unfiltered sky. I am made
of a dark matter now, elemental.
I dance at the edge of all singing and leaving.
I shiver myself to joy.

◇◇◇

Showroom Cadillacs. Soybeans and corn feed. Shipments of ball bearings
packed in Detroit. Scrap iron filings. Two hundred kilos Peruvian cocaine
stashed in a shipment of soap. Olive oil. Crude oil. Blue Mountain coffee
imported from Kingston, flown out, trucked up the Allegheny range. Crate
& Barrel dish sets. Purses from Tiffany's. Things I could never afford.
Knock-offs from Thailand, Myanmar, China. T-shirts from sweat shops
and fair-trade organics all riding along in the same rusty car. Plutonium forged
in a Tennessee factory. Nikes and import Adidas from unnamed factories
south of the Rio Grande. Whole wings of airplanes strapped to the open decks.
Turbines. iPhones. Evergreen cars for the sawblades in Portland. Bound
for the dealerships. Bound for the freightliners leaving the Puget Sound,
blowing their horns at the Golden Gate Bridge. The weight of it. All of it.
Rolling away from its origin, down from the mountain pass, down from
the bankrupted silver mines leaking, down from the Black Hills, down from
the timberline, down from the flatland to finally rest in the sea.

◇◇◇

The road goes on. With or without us.
It writes itself into the walls of our passage, scratches its name
on the shoulders of mountains,
concrete embankments, picnic bench tables,
the tear-away bark of a young summer sapling,
stenciled in four-foot ridiculous tags
on the bridge overlooking the line.
It is written in brandings,
in torn leather scraps of a boat cover, faded tattoos,
in the high-ball train and million-layered skywork,
glimpsed momentarily in clouds.

◇◇◇

Somewhere near Havre the rain disappears.
The beat slows down and the sun spreads two
red parallel flames on the tracks. Weird
benediction. Beautifully there for a moment
and gone. A calico horse bows down
to the barbwire, kissing the stalks of grass.
Darkness comes down as we enter the yard
and I pack up my gear for the bull.
Nothing moves. Only the fishplates
settling cold. I lean to the shadow. I wait.

❖ ❖ ❖

When the Crew Change is finished,
the bull drives by with a floodlight
shocking the walls. Stopping to walk
down the blue forty-eights. I can feel
his boots on the ballast beside me,
searching the rideable wells. All my luck
and starless fate and prayers are his
alone. I know he knows I'm here.
Still, tonight, the flashlight turns.
The air brakes start their slow release.
The U-locks lurch and slam in place
and the whistle redeems me, washed in time,
in the fine-silt clay of the Red River,
washed in the unrelenting wind. It is washed
in the blood of thieves and outlaws,
washed in the wild drunk calls of bandits
and minor dealers and riffraff apostles
and all the ragged crews of my youth.
The ones who ran and the ones who wandered back,
swearing to never return. It is washed
in the words of my father's sermon, my mother's
sermon the same, and I hear it sing

in the mainline metal and curse and anoint
the American prairie and ride my crooked veins.

❖❖❖

Butterfly caught in the backwind, dancing a dead loop.
Friends now, I give him the end of my finger,
shelter him under my shirt.
Pink Floyd plays from a trailer home window.
Tie-dyed curtains. Tall pines drowsy
with sun. Fly fishers casting their lines on the Kootenai,
breaking the rainbows in half.
Boy at a crossing in Libby, Montana. Ten feet away
from my face. I smile and wave
but he stares right though me. Sees only motion and size.
Bats turn soundlessly under the stars.
I sleep in waves, in rocks
and waves. I barely sleep at all.

❖❖❖

Water towers assert themselves on the morning.
Voices arrive out of nowhere, depart,
trail off into other conversations, other music entirely.
A sequence forms. Songs move out of it,
audibly, over the flapping flags, over the pleated greens
and lawn decorations and all the tragic
factories of the Midwest steaming inside my blood.
All the neon bars. All the faded-out
industry logos. Hot rod cars on the downtown strip.
The family-owned wheat farm my grandfather,
during the thirties, hopped trains down to Beaumont,
South Dakota, to work. The men in those days
all clad in the black-and-white sadness of silent films,

sated on hard tack, riding the blinds
where the boilerman shoveled the coal.
Over the tender hearts of their future wives,
dead now. Over the grandchildren selling their land
and the fracking rigs taking their place,
on fire. The country they came from
chasing a dream and the actual dream defined.
Over the shores of silent seas, the massive
unsinkable ships. Over the Iron Range, Driftless,
last great depression and boomtown
closing the mine. Over the Chinese immigrants
dying for nothing, hammering holes in the hearts
of mountains, joining the east and west with a golden spike.

❖❖❖

Dark eye. Darkening into the Cascade Tunnel
I sing myself into a zone. Low down,
sweet and familiar sounds. *Train I ride is ten miles high.*
Train I ride is two miles wide. Ride on,
Babylon, ride. I see the entryway fade to a bright coin,
blue in the circling stone. Sounds are thick
and pictures of gone lives float
on the calcium walls. Gently rocking.
Absolute black. Holding my fingers in front of my face
there is nothing. Only the diesel exhaust
in the airflow, my brother and I
in bunk beds hearing the freight trains buckle
and shift. All night changing
their mile-long loads on the field roads leading away.
We could tell by the whistle if one
was a coal train or one was a mail train
headed down south. We knew by the rhythm
and clack of the joiners, the speed
they were taking the turns. We knew
there was something important inside the sound.

We crawled to the window to look
at the crossing guards flashing their red-blinking light
on the road. Low drone beneath it.
Malt-O-Meal smokestacks leaching off pillars
of heat. We spoke to each other
in whispers, the snore of our father asleep down
the hall. We felt the walls tremble, the weight
of a thing that could sever a man's hand,
cover the distance from New York to Portland,
from ocean to free range. Cut through
the Rockies and prairieland west of us.
Flatten the president's face off
the pennies and nickels we placed on the tracks.

❖ ❖ ❖

You forget your name. You forget your body
has form. Half in dream, half out, you are carried
in memories only, dull shades, consciousness
born to the basal proximities, there for a moment
and gone in the dank hole, gone to the deeper earth,
not really caring whether you live or die.

❖ ❖ ❖

On the north side of Cloudy Pass,
skirting the edge of Mt. Ridley and Sawtooth,
my dad and I hike through the heather with no map,
matching each other step for step,
rock for rock, signaling faintly without words,
hoping to make it downstream before dusk.
I offer the water. He hands me the peanuts
and brushes the circling flies from my back.

❖❖❖

Where are we going? What door are we
entering now? Purely alone
in the long half-hour of turning ourselves to dust. Scraps
of a lost cause, fragments, small unexplainable seeds
of grief and all our futures gone.
I don't want to see beyond the hills,
the crumbling walls of barns,
the great herds of elk and boneyards of cattle
we passed in the Flathead Range.
I want to remain in mystery now, in the musty spiritual dark
of this cave, where nothing is lost,
and nothing begins or ends,
or turns around,
or dissolves in the blood's dark tide.
The river rolls. The ocean throws its tired chain of waves
against the shore. The road goes on,
in darkness, falling rain,
before our birth and after we fade like so much windblown sand,
the light that finally comes
is warm, and all at once,
and blinding.

❖❖❖

Train I ride is ten miles high.
Train I ride is two miles wide.

❖❖❖

Over the single direction of time. Over the now and forever,
the long gone. Over the bright orange Burlington cattle guards

blasting the mule deer clear to the weeds, steam lifting up
from the Washington apple farms, swirling their magnified spells
in my face. Over the grinding gears. Over the endless arrival,
departure of light. The whistle calls us back. It rises from ragweed,
ballast and black tar. It moves us. It carries us home.

IV

PIKE

My grandma remembers the lake-water hitting
the boat. The low back-and-forth of buoyed
weight working to hold up the bodies
inside. Her father removing a worm from
the loose earth, threading the wet pink flesh
with a hook. Dirt on his fingers. The long
bleeding body in agony, curling to feel
its way up the nylon line. Even as the bed nurse
changes the bag, squeezes her arm for
a vein, she remembers the sun-dried cork
in her hands. Clear reverberations through
the bamboo pole as the worm swung over
the psychedelic water and the lure-weight
started to fall. In the distance, a loon's call.
Or was it a boy calling out to his friend
on the dock? The way he said, *Carl. Hey,*
Carl, come here. She remembers the sadness
of that name: *Carl.* Brothers, of course,
and in love in a way she would never be able
to guess. Ladybugs dead in the silk of a cobweb,
eagle wings rasping the air. She watches
the window to take in the autumn trees,
cherry leaves dotting the lawn. She can feel
the long gold trail behind them, dance of
the motor. Her father saying, *Tease it now.*
Bring it to life. She remembers this, yes,
she is sure she remembers. Moon floating over
invisible water. The pole bent double, and, yes,
she is sure: the force pulling harder below.

BELLINGHAM FAIR

for Kerri-Ann

Our last good morning we walked to the fence
where the rides sat hulking like sad imaginations
in the sun, embarrassed and shining,
missing some purer sound.
And the off-season fishermen stood around bow-legged,
testing the Tilt-a-Whirl, Gravitron, briefly
adjusting the gears, replacing the dead bulbs,
sipping from plastic bottles
of Windsor Canadian. You kept your distance.
Jumping the tide pools at Post Point, pulling it off
with your horse-like gait. Ironic in most ways,
wheeling around from behind me,
staring across the bay, saying,
The day is like wide water, without sound,
as if you were stealing the scene from a movie.
Beyond us, the blues of the vanishing islands,
the desiccated fountains, depending on
the light. How so much depended on the light—
the cool clip in the air that night.
Larch trees turning, beginning to bring
the fall. The hands of another man—tattooed,
a stranger—arranging your hips at the edge
of my absences. Rides on the midway, spinning
in concert. The last night any of it mattered. Trying to see
through it. Beyond it. To some other ending.
But only seeing fear, the flavor of gin, the pulse in your hand
wrapped tightly around my wrist. Trying to push out
whatever belief we had in that beauty.
The morning stars. The blue irreducible sea.

ONCE IN THE RODIN GARDEN

I slept under highways. Railroad blankets.
Pale blue sections of tarp. Boathouses.
Scaffold of downtown apartments. Black
clouds above me, the shadows of mountains
like mountains of darkness themselves.
In Paris I slept in the Rodin garden. The fountain
turned off. The pigeons disappeared to their
quiet corners in bushes. I stayed up most nights,
afraid to sleep, listening closely for sounds.
There was one night I heard a couple
make love. They were next to a tree, right there
on the grass. Her breath made me shake.
It was full of so much life. For the next
few days I could hear it in every word I said.
It's October now. Leaves turning orange, red,
brown. Leaves raked in piles on boulevards,
leaves packed in storm drains, leaves
crumbled up in the street. Costumes have gone up
in windows downtown. Pumpkins are piled
on hay bales outside the Safeway. Above me,
an arrow of geese flies off, riding trade winds
from Vancouver Island. What is it inside me
that needs to be leaving, that needs to be
lonely and untouched by wind? This place
where the water dissolves into water,
where cricket-hum rises away from the weeds,
and a silence not unlike the heart is filled.

MUTANTS

Every morning they climbed the embankment
and sat in the willow reeds, waiting for food.
And every morning the old man walked down
the dirt path, carrying a metal bucket of duck-feed
under his arm, pouring the contents out
on the grass. I watched from my window,
or from the playground where I sat in the still swings,
hoping to write. Waiting for a true word
to enter me, or flash momentarily on the dark water
next to the dock. Mostly, it was nothing.
White sand and wind. Small bugs caught
in the spiderwebs hung between chains.
Mostly, I just sat and stared at the water,
at the tallest pines on the opposite shore,
thinking of ripping it out. The way wind
can only push forward. The way silence can only
push back. And in October, when the koi pond
froze, and their mother abandoned them
in the nest, knowing they wouldn't be able
to fly, I watched the man walk down to the reeds
in the dark, putting his hand down flat
on a wood block, letting them pick out the grain.
Once, I wrote, *Light pouring in through the windows
of death's dark cathedral*, and knew it was fake.
Another time, I watched two of the males,
huddled in the first snow, shivering under
the tall oak, and the man standing quietly,
watching the lake. I wrote, *Water and more
water*. I wrote, *One or the other must go.*

RIDING THE HIGHLINE

At first there was only the faint sound of sprinklers hitting the tanker
near my head. The cool rush of semi-trucks leaving the valley. The low
moon climbing the trees. And off in the distance, the endless procession

of Hanjin container cars vanishing into the hills. I was somewhere near
Minot. Hungry. Dehydrated. Doing my best to approximate the hour by
watching the glow on the distant ties (some thirty miles closer to California)

get brighter. I watched the line. Waiting to feel the drum of the engine,
the guttural sound of the Bull car rounding the higher-priority freight.
Maersk. Ying Mang. Piggyback rides for the shipyard in Oakland. Fords

for the dealerships east. I could feel the cold weight. The muscle of diesel
and slack-line beneath me. Air brakes shuddering, starting to wheeze.
And then, as if finding a hole in my body, as if turning a handle and opening

up a door, the new medication cut through. The rails went forward
and backward at once. I could see the divided lines, ox-bowing slowly,
losing themselves in the haze. How even the clouds moving over them

froze. How they backtracked and ended up blending again into darkness.
And how, as a boy in my grandparent's pool, floating with water-wings,
holding my face near the chemical drain in the wall (because it was safer

there, the echoes somehow less exposed), I discovered a bee's nest the size
of a baseball, small enough to cup in my hand, and thought it was strange
to have built one so close to the water. How the waves didn't touch it.

How the pool must never get used. The wash of those river roads, covered
in brightness. Deer bodies rising away from the snow. The mouth of my
grandmother opening, closing, laughing to cover the loss of a name.

The weight of her memory falling like stones through the wrought iron grill
of a drain. Rippling lowly. Slow light returning. Mealworms, prairie dogs,
dark knots of garter snakes, small toads snug in the earth. The smell of my

father's shirt. The smell of the dry florid dust-wind of South Santorini.
The towering, suicidal cliffs of the White Beach. Those breathless
prehistoric pillars of salt rock. Startling blue of the Mediterranean Sea.

Your eyes at the train station lobby on King Street, kissing me awkwardly
once on the forehead and turning forever away. The letter unfolding.
The faint and invisible mist. The pure soul. I could see the green wheel

of time underneath me. It rolled endlessly over the dark horizon. Into
the sheer plains, into the clay fields echoing dawn, breathing the held heat,
smolder of dead fish, nitrogen, hogs ground up in the slaughterhouse plow.

It continued in green waves. Into the one-horse midnight towns. Into
the holes in the hearts of mountains. It became a country. A possible god.
And there in ballast, there in the field beside the train, I could picture

my father bent over the first dog we owned, gone rabid from chewing on
batteries, eyes closed and quivering, shaking her back legs and stiffening up.
Not from the pain but from something more sweet—the prairie beginning

to let itself loose, or the clear unexplainable sound of the sea, when you
hear it as distance behind some hills (the seagulls sit hovering, tipping
their wings just enough so they don't ever have to come down). At first

there was only the static of rain, the sprinklers turned on, and the haze
of a dream I was already leaving behind. But then, I could see how the rails
combined. How they joined at the far edge, wound with the wheat rows,

truckstop sprinklers, pallid lot, bricks in the small tiled sign reading: *Come
Back Soon*. The truckers emerging from claustrophobic blankets, jaded
by landscape, refusing to stretch themselves out, walking horse-like

and lighting the day's first smoke. It was all there. Endless. The hands of my
grandmother braiding themselves to the fields—the bruised veins shivering,
riding the morphine, long-haulers chasing the star-cover west. The sediment

dust in a vacancy, pillowcase, blanket stain, antique sideboard—I saw it
contained in a similar frame, extending in soy fields and spraypainted
billboards forever. Not to say *infinite*, but to go on without it. To endure

without knowing there's anything left. And my bent father, lifting our dog
from her seizure, carrying her over the wet grass into the backyard, pushing
the kitchen knife through. The certain, appropriate action. Now hard

to remember completely. The motion light bleaching the roof of the garage,
the sight of his boots moving over the lawn, the walnut leaves hanging
indifferent as stars. The slow-motion focus. The lack of a sound. I remember

the terry cloth waving alone on the railing. The fly still inside it. The frayed
edge. The small undramatic collection of blood. And my father alone
in the backyard digging, saying nothing, believing he did something good.

POSERS

Outside the bookstore in downtown Seattle
we huddle away from the rain. Two days
out of the mountains and looking to hitchhike
a ride down to Plain. Scrape a few dollars together
for food. Cars move quietly over the road.
Rain beats down on the blue plastic awning
we've jimmy-rigged over our heads. There are
three of us asking for spare change and handouts.
Night falling slowly away from the stores.
The girl named Saturday plays the guitar.
My brother and I sing softly along, working
to keep us in key. We look bedraggled and crazy.
We stagger and weave in the limited range
of the tarp. I think to myself I am not this
hungry. I am not this desperate for any
clean thing. I am only a few more weeks
on the west coast. Living off food stamps,
volunteer work at the Bellingham food shelf.
Squandering yogurt and leftover bread from
the Trader Joe's dumpster on First. I say I am
working to make myself better. Learning
the rhythm and speed of my heart. The same
three chords and the harmony failing. Nodding
along to the sound of my brother's voice.
Trying out the words in my own mouth until
I am finally able to sing.

MERCY SONGS

He heard them in the weight room, in the white
expanse of the courtyard covered in snow,
the way it reminded him always of Sundays,
waking up late in the empty apartment at noon,
pulling his socks on, holding a cold can
of Steele Reserve to his chest. He heard them
in the mess hall, in the empty machine shop walls,
the drone of the late night stations on faith,
the pop of the ping-pong ball in the background,
the gorgeous prayers of Emanuel Paine
when he really got going, when he drowned out
and slipped into tongue. He heard them in heat pipes,
in checkerboard back slaps, dip spit sloshing
around in the can, shuffling decks of cards,
the high-pitched scuff of the bald guard's boot
on the painted-blue concrete floor. The one
they called Tee-Do. The one who wore crosses
and belted out *lowly, my savior* and *sinnerman*
the way Nina Simone had sung it live
at Carnegie Hall in 1965. He heard them
in the stuttering tick of the wall clock, the sound
of a freight train crossing the county line,
the snoring gestures of big Jack Wheeler who shared
the room for a year, who lied about women
he couldn't have slept with, murders he didn't commit.
But mostly, he heard them in the private hours
of waiting to fall asleep, when everyone else was alone
in their dreams and the whole penitentiary seemed
to be floating, like one of those city-sized cruise ships
you take to the Arctic, or Cape of Good Hope,
or those Indian islands with lions and dragons,
where pirates had one time divided their treasures
and slept in the mouths of caves.

SLEEP

In downtown Chicago the vendors are folding
their boards up, tossing the leftover scraps in the trash.
Dogs in the alleyway sniffing a drain spout.
Cars headed home and the sun sinking down
like a fiery coin in the lake. My brother says maybe
the shelter will take us in. Maybe we ride on the El
up to Evanston, camp on the grounds of a fancy estate.
A pale light burns in the Sears Tower windows,
sparking electric, as if there were pieces of diamond
being shattered inside. A few lonely sailboats search
the dividing line, turning their rudders in,
slacking the jib lines for shore. We ask for directions,
a few bucks for nachos. Whatever sounds easy
for someone to give. The night is beginning
to stretch out its dark wing. Carry us into
the wind. We name a few friends we can barely
remember. Search through our Facebook accounts
at the mall. Our calls go unanswered. A thin rain
is starting to darken the sidewalk around us,
forcing us under a ledge. With nothing to guide us,
we slide through the open emergency door on the El.
Ride down to Ashland and Sixty-Third,
pick out some pears from the corner store dumpster.
Most of the Southside deserted at midnight.
Burn barrels flash in the doorways of recent foreclosures.
Can pickers dig though recycling bins on the curb.
We follow the track-line, hop a few chain-link fences.
Set up our bags in a back-alley entrance where truckers
deliver supplies to a bar. No one in earshot.
We lean on the bolted door, whispering down at the shadows
between us now. Taking our turns with the knife.

THE CLOUDMAKER'S KEY

Crows Point. Two miles west of the Burlington yard.
Slumped on a pallet and water-stained mattress,
needling crayfish heads to a hook. *This life*, he tells me,
is one of those fake plastic rocks in the garden
you break with a hammer to get out
the key. Meaning, when he was younger
his dad used to lock all the doors, made him sleep
in the fort at the neighboring farm. Meaning,
once, he dismembered a pipe-trapped squirrel,
made slope of the tail and tasted
the brain. Meaning, even the soul has a definite shape,
or a way of removing itself from the world.
And beneath him the dirt split to welcome
the flames. And above him the stars
became haloed in pulses, these circular rainbows
he thought he could touch. And at one point
the over-bright sheen in his eyes
went flat as the sewer drain walled with graffiti signs,
oversized penises skewering dragons, a carpet
of dead carp, bullet shells, double A batteries
strung onto wires like beads. And into that darkness,
sidling forward in drowned undulations,
extending his arms to the trees like an eagle,
the bones of some unknown animal sharpened—
We enter the tubes of this goldmine, he tells me.
We enter this darkness alone.

HEAT STROKE IN REDDING

We've been without water for fifteen hours.
Parked in a yard with the patient rotation of sun
moving over our packs. No shade. Nothing but
scrub brush and white rocks dotting the tracks.
Small birds hopping from train car to train car,
searching the Hanjin containers for grain.
We breathe slow, intentional breaths. Huddle
our backs in the foot-wide shadow this rusty
container wall casts. Propping our heads up.
Wetting our hair with the rainwater left in
a heat-warped bottle of Sprite. Neither of us
can believe we are fading. Stars in our eyes
and the constant humidity. Stuttering. Slurring
our S's and T's. He says he remembers a time
we were kids. Seven or eight then, sleeping in
bunk beds. One of us waking up sick in the night
from a potluck dinner at church. Throwing up
over the other one's head. How Mom wouldn't
tell us which one it had been. How she only just
smiled and let us imagine the victim was always
ourselves. Left to the other one's poor choice
of meatloaf. The one chicken nugget gone bad.
We laugh. I offer the sleeve of the rainwater T-shirt.
Run it across his burned lips, the scab that's
beginning to crack. We say we can make it
a few more hours. We need to keep talking,
telling the stories that make us remember, lead us
away from the walls of the car. I say if he
passes out first I will carry him. Over the rocks
and fields of bleached earth. Over the walnut
groves covered in lime. *You'll carry me?* he says,
smiling a little. He flexes his arm so the blood
will move faster. He promises me the same.

SEVEN-DAY FAST

Now I forget what I wanted to say about hunger.
The tree's sharp arrangement of lines
on the white sky, clusters of off-shooting
branches dissolving among them
like outdated scans of the brain.
Faded by sunlight, or disuse, or whatever.
I barely imagine by what. The gathering
dust on the shoebox they wait in.
Filed away for a future appointment
with some other specialist, talking of
networks, compatible pathways,
unsourced receptors, the closest
approximate rate of attrition. They talk
with the same sympathetic restraint
used for death. We see the sterility first,
predictions unfolding in ribbons
of uncharted highways beyond
other skies. We use metaphors
like this. We say the spirit is more
than the critical mass. We say prayers
are reflected in atoms, in snowflakes
freezing, in magnified raindrops.
We say there is no way of knowing
the will. The hand held flat to the palm reader's
always astonished tones. We say dreams.
A series of blackouts, minor strokes.
We say there is more than the body's
measurable electrics. The forgotten
children who stand at the bedrail,
showing us pictures of speedboats and horses,
our own selves posing with tulips and lilacs
in front of our whitewashed homes.
We say the soul. The out-riding weather
inside us. The down-pouring water
that runs from the mountain, that sleeps

in the frozen beet field, that denies
this hunger, that sings in the blood.

WOLF HEAVEN

In the last letter you wrote me, sealed in castor wax,
mailed from somewhere in Hungary I couldn't
make out—the last page yellowed and signed
in your blood, as you always did then, from the side
of your thumb or the pale stretch under your thigh—
you wrote, *Love is a distance, failed by time*,
and went on to describe how the Gaudi cathedral
was melting, how the human statues that lined
the streets of Las Ramblas could hold so perfectly still
there was no way to know they were breathing.
Nothing is permanent here, you wrote, *but nothing is lost*.
In the bleached light of those infinite winters,
I drove to my weekend job at the parks department,
clearing the sidewalk in front of the depot,
shoveling entryways, salting the roads. How purely
the cold made a claim on the body. How slowly the gold
in the hoarfrost fell to the landlines and bent stalks
of corn. If telling you made any difference.
If hearing your name in the high-liner fences,
jaw-harp harmonicas, moans of the train.
I think of the night you did acid in Dennison,
frozen and throwing up medicine, dragging the mud
from your boots on the bed. Or the night we went
driving around on the service roads, finding the bones
of a wolf in the ditch. How weirdly the skull sat shining
in the moonlight. And how quietly I held you then,
watching the tree shadows rise on the downed blinds,
talking of floodlights and wolf eyes and what
a strange gift it would be to be dead. Those moments
are silence inside me now. Lost in the snow piles north
of the yard. And what can I call them? A phony rose?
A frozen carnation? A thing to keep sealed
in a clear plastic box in the fridge? It could have been
anyone, taking me down to the train bridge, pouring
the India ink on my shin. Walking the deer trails

back to the spillway, climbing the guardrail, touching
our tongues to the bars. *Not to love*, you wrote, *but to learn
not to trust the deception. It's this life or nothing.
To die with intention. To leave something blue in your skin.*

TITANIC

The spirit is not broken by cold. By the blowing snow
or the shattered bone, the pale shade of your grandmother's face
as she wanders away from the world. The spirit
is broken by something else. More common
to the root. Dithering light in the blood bank lobby.
Lull of shame in your younger brother's voice.
Waiting in line at the Sundance Six for the Saturday
matinée. Hoping to sleep in the dark back row
where the ticket-boy might not check. Spilled pop.
Week-old Sour Patch Kids on the concrete under
our shoes. When we found our seats in the crowded theater,
the strangers sitting beside us moved away
because of the smell. The dirt on our hands.
The strain in our eyes from going the last two nights
without sleep. We could hear them muttering
under their breath as the lights came down
and the screen lit up with the opening shot of the sea.

NORTH SHORE RECOVERY

There's nothing to see here. Only the faint red
tower light blinking. A series of hoofprints
dissolving in trees. Clouds curl up in the heat of my breathing
and a man on a snowmobile glides through the darkness,
carving the shore on the far other side
of the lake. Wrapped in a thick coat, black-tinted helmet,
what is he searching those distances for?
Where is he going with so much
intention? Gunning the belt over wind drifts
and ditch berms, riding alone through the cattail patches
and emptied-out sloughs of the night.
The birds have quit feeding. The squirrels are somewhere asleep
in their rotted-out holes. The moon lets the stars
do the bulk of the shining, and wind sidles down in the crowns
of the pines. I imagine the fear
in the cold hearts of muskies, slowed to a suicide pace
at the springs. Hearing the grind of that overhead engine.
Staring up once in a while at cracks
where a small strip of brightness comes through.

SPLITTING A FORTY WITH ANT B

I grew up right here by the tracks. We had a nice
little homestead. A neighborhood. I like to come
back here. I got my privacy here. I got a beer and
a tree-shadow. And the bugs ain't too bad. I had
a guidance counselor in Community College who
told me I slipped through the cracks. She said,
I'll tell you what's happened, you slipped through
the cracks. You imagine my face when she said that?
I felt small. I just about vanished. They used to have
lions down here by the river. They were taking them
down to Chicago. Waiting for one of the zoos to get
finished. Built them a cage with a barbwire fence.
I think it was supposed to be a *temporary* enclosure.
Like a one-time thing. But they left them for most
of the summer. Beautiful creatures. In August,
we found them just sitting there, watching us back
through the bars. Kickboxing bag for the babies
to play with. Sharpen their claws on. A family of
lions. The male would always get giant erections.
Like the size of your arm. Like he wanted to eat you
for breakfast. I lived with my grandma and grandpa
in Northtown. My grandpa was a bad alcoholic.
He worked for the government, pouring cement.
He owned the river. I told him I'd come back to
Northtown and kill him. I was serious, too. But no
one will love you for killing your grandpa, so I
drank in the basement, skipped school and that.
At the end of the summer we checked on the cages.
The trains had been loaded. The lions all gone.

NORTHTOWN CHOIR

When the stories are finished, the fire burned down
to a puddle of glittering coals, the guy they call
Spider Eyes picks up a stick and starts smacking
the side of a log. Doling a rhythm out, picking up
tempo and stomping his boots in the sand. My brother
comes in with a railroad spike on a turned-over
bucket of Schwan's. Ringing the bass notes clear.
Holding the backbeat. Stain of the sugar and swan logo
faded forever ago by the rain. The dog begins whining.
The dude from Montana we only just met begins
working a long pair of spoons. Beatboxing
awkwardly, blurting out lyrics and grinding his way
through the lines. The dark trees nodding. The black
snakes waiting like pills on the Northtown strings.
I imagine the scene at a distance. A gang of marauders.
A wandering posse of infantrymen at the end of a third
world war. Not the two blond sons of a pastor,
the son of a physics professor from Phoenix, the son
of an auto mechanic who beat him and gave him permission
to run away young. Not the fear we are only
pretending. The faded white scar over Spider Eyes' eye.
Not the hunger we've carried together. The wild
and lonely American moon we've already left behind.

MINNESOTA ROADS

Dawn and I'm driving the back-country dairies
and hayricks on North 64, my brother asleep
on the window beside me. Radio tuned
to an alt-country station they stream
out of Walker-Laporte. Fog over everything.
Wheels and ditch grass. Broken machinery
rusting away in the yards. Satellites shine
now and then in the lifting dark. Headlights align
with the fences and trail off, haunted
like fishing boats trolling the point.
Everything stalks to the edge of the morning
and waits. Even our car seems to slide
on the cusp of a barely invisible screen.
Hinting at some kind of wilder country the silos
have always kept hidden from view—
squatting an open air flatcar in Portland,
opening tin cans of stewed prunes and tuna fish,
fireworks blooming the eastern Montana sky.
Thinking of Olaf alone in the mountains now.
Kerri-Ann living on food stamps in Bellingham.
Severson army-bound. Zeidlhack dead.
Somewhere near Wilmar the sun hits the trees
and my brother wakes up to the glare. Townes
on the radio. Crows on the power lines passing beside us
in waves. *I dreamt of a mutated cowboy,*
he tells me. *A man without fingers, but still
having hands.* I pass him the rest of our Zig Zags
and shaker. He takes out the rumpled-up atlas
and rolls down the window to let in some air.

SECRET AIR

I know no god. No ghost. No code that turns
the burning engine back. I know a highway,
field, stars above the sleeping corn. The river
rolls. The world spins alone. We are not promised
love like this. We don't decide what brighter
angel comes, what water climbs the banks.
It could have been a different year, a better pill,
a weird forgotten dream, a song I heard behind
the neighbor's door, the barking dog again.
But it was you. The only one to make it last.
To hold my head like this. To lead me back
inside myself. To know. To be. The sadness
of a summer horse unbridled on a hill. Departing
air, the farmhouse crumbling in the wind.
I could have lived a hundred lives and never
known a real kiss. I could have gone without
your winter stars, your streetlight-tinted
breath. But it was you. The one who made
the darkness real. The highway blue. The rose's
hollow thorn. I know we die alone, in separate
rooms, with canceled eyes and some disease
inside our hearts—but still, we knew a love
like this. We knew. And all the nights I sleep
in someone else's arms, the rhythmic dark,
the drifty San Francisco nights I wander with
the crowd, from here to there to somewhere else,
the Safeway lines and subway lines and traffic
streaming west—I return again. I remember you
and only you like this. Your careless grip,
your pale eyes beside me in the corn. The sheet
of plywood for a bed. It is what is. Among
the cricket's song, the muddy river rising up
the banks. I meet you there. I turn to hold you
in the secret air that only you will know.

CRY OF THE LOON

for Roald Carlson 1925–2015

Sundown. Kabekona Lake. I paddle the fishing boat
out to the drop-off and wait for the deepening light.
Mosquitoes fly lazily over the oarlocks.
Clouds turn purple and darken to gold.
Sailboats drift under eddies of stalled wind
and loons call wildly out from the cattails,
sending their terrifying cries to the night.
We must remember the blue of the water is only
the surface reflecting the sky. The weight
of our bodies the leftover seed of some violent burn
at the core. The rails run out but the wheels
keep turning. The fire goes down but the winter
keeps pushing its sap to the towering pines.
We see through the window but don't hear
the chorus of waves coming down on the sand,
the bodies of sailors and freightliners
dragged down, sea creatures yet to be born.
We are not put on earth to remember the dead.
We are not given access to ways we will suffer,
what light might become us, or how it will end.
We are given a few dreams, a few nights of wonder—
a whisper, a shiver, a miracle chance to be held
in another one's arms. The day goes on fading.
The night goes on beating its drums to the hideaway stars.
We are given a few years to laugh at the danger.
To break ourselves down in the service of joy. And then,
we are floating. The water is black. And our quiet Alumacraft
fishing boat carries us farther and farther from shore.

DUNDAS

I am but a stranger here, Heaven is my home
—*Traditional Lutheran Hymn*

Even the interstate cries out of silence, hovering under
the floodlights and puddles of gasoline burning the moon.
Someone is leaving this city forever. And someone is
driving the Sauvie Island beaches where girls walk naked
from their night shadows anticipating more than the scars
of desire. Anticipating wind rising up through their bodies
like song. Because despite what we think, we are always
returning to an outfield in Dundas, Minnesota, where we
stand among tree groves and rotted-out trains and watch
balls sail over the fence in the other direction. Tell me,
where do we go from here then, stranger? Lost in the wind drift
and catalogue highways. Stilled in the brain with invisible
cities. Girls in Portland returning this hunger. Walking
the Hawthorne with wings in their hair. Even the gilded
madonnas in Brooklyn are crying for their hearts to be
opened. Sleeping in gutter-punk squats in Berlin, empty
cathedrals where nobody prays, where tourists reach
for the black hand of Jesus, sweat-stained and dulled
to a nub. Even the dogs on the streets of Chicago.
Even the bird on the burning streets of Santorini, picking
a crust of bread. There's a reason we only move farther
from Dundas. There's a reason we don't see the true leaf
looking at a eucalyptus grove, a eucalyptus tree, a single leaf
hanging in the backdrop forever. Because beauty is never
as clear as the sound—the headlight, the half-light we see
in a dream. The mind wants to move in a circle, return
to the lines it remembers the best, find itself riding
a series of high short notes through the ceiling and off
in the ether. The soul says go clear. The heart says
go back to the first cry and do it again. The mind only
spins in between. A three-headed lizard. A house cat
with nothing to do but stalk yardbirds and chew

on its tail. There's another thing too. Something
we don't have a word for. If God were enough, we keep
saying, but it's not. And anyone who's seen it will tell you
there's nothing but light and space and oblivion at the end.
Nothing but the same luck ruined by meaning. By living
too close to the words. The emptied-out backstreet.
The small white ball in the field lights covered in flies.
The freshly mowed grasses. The visible parts of Orion.
The cricket-sounds building the dark other side of the fence.
And in Portland, where girls walk shyly from winter.
Their imperfect habits. Move ceaselessly over the Steel Bridge,
crossing the river on bicycles, cruising the night roads, hovering
over the oil drums piled on rail-set barges below. All skin-black,
shivering rust in the glare. A reed of pure ecstasy pressed to your lips.
Returning in floodlights and black water shining and song.

O DAY FULL OF GRACE

for Elizabeth Wee 1909–2009

> Farmers stood in their yards outside the city watching as the boiling black clouds continued their journey . . . like many steel drums rolling across the floor of a distant palace . . . looking straight up, one saw what appeared to be a patchwork quilt with the yarn-ties being pulled out one by one. . . . by now, the roar was so loud that people knew it was not a freight train they heard.
>
> —*from The Great Fergus Falls, Minnesota Cyclone of June 22, 1919*

She sings to remember. Tipping her head back,
letting her fingers go limp on the keys.
Humming the lyrics and handing me photographs,
black-and-white faces with names on the backs
of them, standing up once at the window
to look at the pink-tinted cherry leaves fall.
Daddy on Saturday. 1903. The man is dressed
in a clean-pressed suit, Stetson and briefcase,
wing tip shoes. Fourteen years old
at the train station waiting for someone to carry
his bags. Behind him the prairie dissolves
into cloud and the tall individual grass blades
rush like an eyelash of crop dust, a shiver
of heatwave hovering there on the rails.
It came like rain, she says. *Nothing at first.*
We thought it was only a train. The single-room
church I'm imagining now is abandoned,
obliterated, pissed in by teenagers, littered
with pop bottles, scattered across those fields
like so much dust. It came like a wave, she says.
Like a ship horn's blare. Like a street sweeper
pushing his broom to a rhythm. Like one dog's
bark as the evening arrives, the glow of a town
in the distance approaching. It came like a song,
like everything else comes: imperfectly, lacking
apologies, heaving, surprised by its sudden

existence. I try not to think of the basement
she prayed in. The floorboards, shingles above
her dissolved. Crosses and curtain rods launched
from the windows, being pulled through
the suddenly vacated doors. I try not to think
of the tulips and lilacs arranged in bouquets
on the mantel. Black-nickel hailstones pleating
the flatland, stunned by the sound of it, severing
lone oaks with telephone wires gone stray.
The intricate bloom of their absence inside her.
The days she remembered in hearing some hymn,
where it took her, a serious face in the fog,
a man standing still on the platform in Fargo,
the already gone train leaving its whistle inside him,
a voice calling *datter* and *datter* to one small tree,
one flooded foundation, one beet pile sloughing
off steam in the hot night, holding the earth's
heat in. I imagine the song. Not language itself
but the secret it's keeping. Rotating wheel
of seed in the choir loft, vanishing over the corn.
She smiles then, tracing the face of the man
with a finger, searching the eyes in the blown-out grain.
Naming a series of nowhere Dakota towns,
junked Fords, rusted-out bicycles marking the dirt
roads of Havre, Montana. *He never got west*
of the mountains, she tells me. *Died of pneumonia*
and lung complications before we were able
to leave. The distance he traveled from Bergen
to Brooklyn. From Brooklyn to Cleveland.
From Saint Cloud to Fargo. From Fargo to one
insignificant single-room church at the Chippewa
end of the prairie. The song is the only thing
left to contain it. The only thing cherished.
The only thing able to draw back a hair from
her own father's face and remember. To cull
from the darkness the sound of my name. To dream
without waking at night to the parking lot view
of the cherry leaves falling forever. Bright sheen

of cow brains embossing the barbwire. Catfish
in rain gutters, cats on the clotheslines with pebbles
of plate glass inside them. And into that ether,
that eerie light spread over everything not torn down—
salt-sanded shingles and beer bottles dropped
in the shape of a star on the lawn—her piano
untouched, her breathing machine just a rustle
of plastic, a moan. In the dim halls of the Dundas
Retirement Home, I watched her become so thin
I could look at the blood press a blue vein
out of her. Drag her around the assisted living
grounds without purpose. A song on the piano
for no one. A station on television seen right
through. In the photo, a man with a darkness
behind him. Ducks in the foreground, horses
in harness, kids carrying boxes of cargo from
train car to train car, and someone anonymous,
maybe the conductor, maybe a curious passenger,
checking the U-joints, residue flakes on the firebox,
some unforeseeable light in the distance approaching,
a look in his eye like the prairie was some kind
of ocean he knew would obey him. I thought if
I sang. My hand to those ventricles, tracing
the bulge of formaldehyde backward. Over
the loose folds. Over the pale blue river of days.
I thought if I knelt by the bed rail, humming.
Leading the melody back to the clay. The way
it could leave her preservative body intact: a vestige,
a vacated doll. The way her white blazer kept
threatening breath. Her face gone slack, somehow
more defined. More controlled by the bones.
The lids of her eyes unable to close up completely.
A slight gleam lingering there. Wanting her lips
to reanimate, not to reanimate. Simply to vanish.
To drift in the same cloud, the same destroyed field
she wandered in searching for signs of whatever
remained. Living dogs whining in whole other
counties. Hogs in the granaries. Cow bodies

bloated with chickenfeed sewn to their skin.
Sheered birds floundering, featherless lumps
of blood. *Things you would never believe.*
And out in the car-littered ditches—a thin
strand of straw stuck straight through an elm.
The feeling of touching it. Of breaking it clean
in her hand. How easy it must have seemed,
in that impossible moment, to steal away
on a ribbon of highway, to evacuate her body,
to simply disappear. To become like the fields
she dreamed of escaping. The stain of that picture,
the emptiness there. To become like the song
and the silence inside it, the speed of those roads
in the wake of it leaving, that horrible beautiful sound.

HOLES IN THE MOUNTAIN

Even the dead rats in the alleys of Oxford,
heads crushed and tossed in a trash bag,
left to fester behind the fence, are waiting
for crows to divide them, to carry their bodies
away. And if not crows, or the street pigeons
picking a leg bone, then the broom
of a street sweeper keeping a rhythm
to one of the tunes in his head. Or the wind
as it funnels the dust in a mini-tornado
above him. Because it isn't enough
to say God is the speed of the wheel
that turns the sky, or that God is the distance
between two trains, hurtling at the same speed
toward you. It doesn't matter what stories we use
to explain these impossible themes—
they will always turn fake or explode
in our faces. On Mount St. Helens
the fires went into the roots of the oldest pines,
smoldered and stayed in the coals for a month
before burning the farms on the opposite side
of the mountain. They found this out later,
tracking a mouse through a network
of intricate caves. We used to have ways
of explaining our failures. Now all we do
is erase them by spreading the veils of blame
so thin. The scars on our hands are only around
to remind us: don't grow old in yourself,
don't get lost in this scrimmage. Because even
death, in its marble skies and free-wheeling borders,
is an art of remembering everything over.
And although the soul is a joke we tell
to the part of ourselves we can touch,
it's only because the soul is a fire, and laughs
at our sorrow, and has already survived us.

ACKNOWLEDGMENTS

Thank you to the editors of the following magazines in which some of these poems first appeared:

Adroit: "Wolf Heaven";
The Arkansas International: "Riding the Highline," "North Shore Recovery";
Best New Poets: "Thresher," "Rail";
Blackbird: "Where the Feeling Deserts Us," "Mercy Songs";
BOAAT: "Northtown Choir";
Boxcar Poetry Review: "Bellingham Fair";
Button: "Cry of the Loon";
Drunken Boat: "Mutants";
Forklift Ohio: "After Havre," "Seven-Day Fast";
Linebreak: "Depression";
The Lumberyard: "The Fog and the Sound";
Miracle Monocle: "Oaks";
The Missouri Review: "Holes in the Mountain," "Sunshine Liquidators," "Jesse James Days," "Bolinas," "The Boy's Head";
Narrative Magazine: "King," "Fly Fishing," "Sleep," "Minnesota Roads";
New England Review: "Rail";
The Paris American: "Steampipe";
Phantom: "The Cloudmaker's Bag";
Ploughshares: "Once in the Rodin Garden";
PNR (British): "Thresher";
The Southern Review: "Pike";
Third Coast: "Crystal Meth";
32 Poems: "The Cloudmaker's Key";
TriQuarterly: "Dundas."

"After Havre" was featured in the documentary film *Riding the Highline.*

"American Freight" is for Danny, Scout, Ant B, Travis, Maya, Brent and Brent, and all the strangers who offered me friendship and grace while I was traveling.

Thank you to the institutions that provided financial support during the completion of this book: the MacDowell Colony, the University of Wisconsin-Madison's Creative Writing Program, *The Missouri Review*, the Dorothy Sargent Rosenberg Fund, the Breadloaf Writers' Conference, the Sewanee Writers' Conference, and Stanford University's Wallace Stegner Fellowship Program.

Special thanks to Eavan Boland, Ken Fields, W. S. Di Piero, Nick Flynn, Campbell McGrath, Dorianne Laux, Tobias Wolff, Adam Johnson, Maurice Manning, Andrew Hudgins, Tom Sleigh, Ron Wallace, Jesse Lee Kercheval, Amaud Johnson, Amy Quan Barry, Michael Dennis Browne, J. J. Murphy, and Lorrie Moore for your generous mentorship and support.

Many thanks to Peter Conners, Robert Bly, Speer Morgan, Jamaal May, Laura Kasischke, Adam Latham, George David Clark, Ron Martin-Dent, Sandy Knight, Aaron Barrell, Gregory Donovan, Tarfia Faizullah, Matt Hart, Natalie Diaz, Rick Barot, Patty Paine, Tom Jenks, Carol Edgarian, and everyone at BOA Editions for your encouragement and anagogical vision.

My deepest love and gratitude to Catherine Pond, Josh Kalscheur, Austin Smith, Christopher Kempf, Gayle Walsworth, Solmaz Sharif, Mario Chard, Laura Romeyn, Edgar Kunz, Cate Lycurgus, Noah Warren, Hugh Martin, Brandon Courtney, Malachi Black, William Brewer, Jacques Rancourt, Nancy Reddy, Louisa Diadato, Shanley Jacobs, Keith Leonard, Kristiana Kahakauwila, Ross Gay, Keith Ekiss, Michael McGriff, Tony Marra, Miriam Bird Greenberg, Greg Wrenn, Jessica Langan-Peck, Jack Schiff, Marymorgan Vegdahl-Crowell, Seth Thomas, Nathan Barnard, Noah Greene, the Bergman family, the Erickson family, and Holden Village.

This book is dedicated to my parents, Morris Wee and Kristine Carlson, and my dear brothers, Anders and Olaf. I couldn't have written these words without you.

ABOUT THE AUTHOR

Kai Carlson-Wee was born in Minneapolis, Minnesota. He received his BA from the University of Minnesota and his MFA from the University of Wisconsin-Madison. His poetry has appeared in *Ploughshares, Best New Poets, TriQuarterly, Gulf Coast,* and *The Missouri Review,* which awarded him the 2013 Editor's Prize. His photography has been featured in *Narrative Magazine* and his poetry film, *Riding the Highline,* has screened at film festivals across the country. A former Wallace Stegner Fellow, he lives in San Francisco and is a lecturer at Stanford University.

BOA EDITIONS, LTD.
THE A. POULIN, JR. NEW POETS OF AMERICA SERIES

No. 1   *Cedarhome*
         Poems by Barton Sutter
         Foreword by W. D. Snodgrass

No. 2   *Beast Is a Wolf with Brown Fire*
         Poems by Barry Wallenstein
         Foreword by M. L. Rosenthal

No. 3   *Along the Dark Shore*
         Poems by Edward Byrne
         Foreword by John Ashbery

No. 4   *Anchor Dragging*
         Poems by Anthony Piccione
         Foreword by Archibald MacLeish

No. 5   *Eggs in the Lake*
         Poems by Daniela Gioseffi
         Foreword by John Logan

No. 6   *Moving the House*
         Poems by Ingrid Wendt
         Foreword by William Stafford

No. 7   *Whomp and Moonshiver*
         Poems by Thomas Whitbread
         Foreword by Richard Wilbur

No. 8   *Where We Live*
         Poems by Peter Makuck
         Foreword by Louis Simpson

No. 9   *Rose*
         Poems by Li-Young Lee
         Foreword by Gerald Stern

No. 10   *Genesis*
         Poems by Emanuel di Pasquale
         Foreword by X. J. Kennedy

No. 11   *Borders*
         Poems by Mary Crow
         Foreword by David Ignatow

No. 12   *Awake*
         Poems by Dorianne Laux
         Foreword by Philip Levine

No. 13   *Hurricane Walk*
         Poems by Diann Blakely Shoaf
         Foreword by William Matthews

No. 14   *The Philosopher's Club*
         Poems by Kim Addonizio
         Foreword by Gerald Stern

No. 15   *Bell 8*
         Poems by Rick Lyon
         Foreword by C. K. Williams

No. 16   *Bruise Theory*
         Poems by Natalie Kenvin
         Foreword by Carolyn Forché

No. 17   *Shattering Air*
         Poems by David Biespiel
         Foreword by Stanley Plumly

No. 18   *The Hour Between Dog and Wolf*
         Poems by Laure-Anne Bosselaar
         Foreword by Charles Simic

No. 19   *News of Home*
         Poems by Debra Kang Dean
         Foreword by Colette Inez

No. 20   *Meteorology*
         Poems by Alpay Ulku
         Foreword by Yusef Komunyakaa

No. 21   *The Daughters of Discordia*
         Poems by Suzanne Owens
         Foreword by Denise Duhamel

No. 22   *Rare Earths*
         Poems by Deena Linett
         Foreword by Molly Peacock

No. 23   *An Unkindness of Ravens*
         Poems by Meg Kearney
         Foreword by Donald Hall

No. 24   *Hunting Down the Monk*
         Poems by Adrie Kusserow
         Foreword by Karen Swenson

No. 25   *Big Back Yard*
         Poems by Michael Teig
         Foreword by Stephen Dobyns

No. 26   *Elegy with a Glass of Whiskey*
         Poems by Crystal Bacon
         Foreword by Stephen Dunn

No. 27   *The Eclipses*
         Poems by David Woo
         Selected by Michael S. Harper

No. 28   *Falling to Earth*
         Poems by Tom Hansen
         Foreword by Molly Peacock

❖ ❖ ❖

COLOPHON

BOA Editions, Ltd., a not-for-profit publisher of poetry
and other literary works, fosters readership and appreciation of
contemporary literature. By identifying, cultivating, and publishing both
new and established poets and selecting authors of unique literary talent,
BOA brings high-quality literature to the public.
Support for this effort comes from the sale of its publications,
grant funding, and private donations.

❖ ❖ ❖

*The publication of this book is made possible, in part,
by the support of the following patrons:*

Anonymous
Angela Bonazinga & Catherine Lewis
Chris & DeAnna Cebula
Peter & Aimee Conners
Jack & Gail Langerak
Melanie & Ron Martin-Dent
Joe McElveney
Boo Poulin
Deborah Ronnen & Sherman Levey
Steven O. Russell & Phyllis Rifkin-Russell
William Waddell & Linda Rubel
Michael Waters & Mihaela Moscaliuc